Ava and Aaron's Christmas story in rhyme

Mariana Books
Rhyming Series
Book 5 Seasons

By
Roger Carlson

Ava's eyes were glued to the window,
waiting for the first sign of snow;
Aaron was reading an Enid Blyton story,
sprawled out on his bed below.

"Ava, you've been sitting there since 7a.m.,"
Aaron said, looking up from his book.
"Come on, let's play a board game and
check back later for another look."

1

Ava shook her head and said,
"I know it will snow today."
She was not going to give up,
even if she watched all day.

It *had* to snow today,
it was Christmas Eve after all;
she wanted to have a white Christmas
and a giant snowman that stood tall.

Aaron went back to reading,
while Ava continued to look out.
She saw something soft land before her;
it was a snowflake - without a doubt!

"IT'S SNOWING! IT'S SNOWING!"
shrieked Ava, hanging out the window;
Mom stuck her head out from the kitchen
and smiled at Ava from below.

"Hi my little monkey," Mom said.
"You got the weather right!"
Ava smiled down at Mom,
full of joy at the snowy sight.

"Let it snow for a bit," said Mom.
"Then you can go outside to play;
please come downstairs first,
we're going somewhere today."

Ava and Aaron ran down
the stairs
as Mom put on her hat.
"Come on you two, grab
your coats,
you're going to need
that."

"Mom, where are we going?"
asked Aaron, as he put on his shoe.
Mom smiled mysteriously and said,
"I have a surprise for you."

5

They drove for half an hour,
Aaron and Ava were about to explode;
with each guess, Mom said no;
she just smiled and kept her eyes on the road.

Then, they heard a familiar noise,
and Aaron looked up to see;
a great big airplane flying low -
then he knew what the surprise would be.

"Mom, are we going to the airport?"
Aaron guessed as he bounced up and down;
Mom laughed and said, "Yes we are!
Guess who's back in town?"

7

Arrival Gate

Ava and Aaron jumped out of the car,
and ran fast to the arrival gate;
they were so excited
that they could hardly wait.

8

Finally, they spotted Dad
wheeling his two suitcases out;
he turned in their direction,
as soon as he heard them shout.

Arrival Gat

"Monkey! Munchkin!
What a nice surprise!
What are you doing here?"
Dad said with delight in his eyes.

10

"So I see," said Dad with a smile
as he gave Mom a big kiss.
"Monkey, Munchkin, catch me up -
tell me everything I missed."

12

After lunch, the four of them went out
to build a giant snowman.
While Dad and Ava made the body,
Mom and Aaron began to plan.

13

Dad and Ava rolled three snowballs:
one big, one medium, one small;
they stacked them on top of each other
carefully, so they wouldn't fall.

14

They gave the snowman Dad's old scarf
and made his hands from twigs;
they gave him a carrot for a nose,
and used buttons to make him smile big!

15

After making snow angels,
they had a big snowball fight;
then they ate Christmas Eve dinner,
and then they all said goodnight.

Ava and Aaron hung up their stockings;
they hoped they'd get some treats;
then they put out milk and cookies,
for Santa and his reindeers to eat.

Dad came upstairs and tucked them in,
Ava and Aaron fell asleep so quick;
then Ava awoke early the next day,
and ran to awake Aaron, he was sleeping
like a brick.

They ran down in excitement,
in their Christmas sweaters and socks;
they saw their presents under the tree,
box upon box upon box!

19

They saw small presents, medium ones
and a couple of large ones too;
Mom and Dad laughed at their excitement
as Ava and Aaron took in the view.

Aaron got a big train set;
he grinned from ear to ear;
Ava got a beautiful ballet dress,
since she was starting classes next year.

They unwrapped all their presents,
as they laughed aloud with glee;
Santa had given them everything,
and some surprises, they could see.

They drank hot chocolate,
watched a Christmas movie on the TV;
then it was time for dinner,
so Mom brought out the giant turkey.

They had stuffing and mashed potatoes,
served with delicious gravy;
cranberry sauce, roasted vegetables
and their favorite desserts so savory!

Mom made Christmas pudding,
apple pies and a tasty plum cake;
their plates were soon piled full,
with more than they could take.

When it started getting dark,
and they were full of food;
Ava and Aaron were getting tired,
But they were in a happy mood.

"Dad," said Ava sleepily,
"I'm glad you're here too;
I asked Santa for many things,
but first I wanted him to bring you."

"Yeah Dad," said Aaron with a smile,
"I'm glad you're here too;
it's best when we're together
and it wouldn't be Christmas
without you."

The family of four sat by the fire,
huddled under a blanket;
this *had* been the best Christmas,
as good as it could get.

29

Santa looked down and smiled;
his beard twinkled in the moonlight;
love is a wonderful thing, he thought,
as he vanished out of sight.

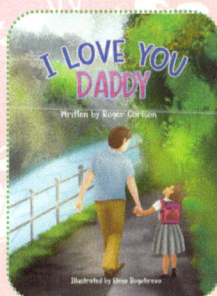

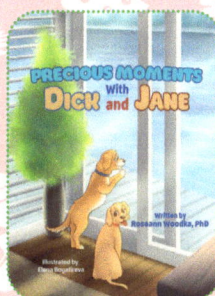

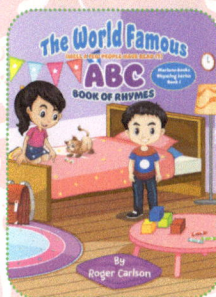

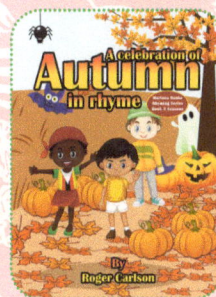
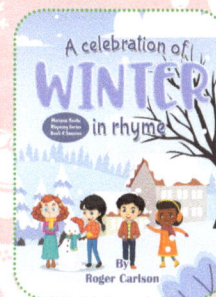

WAYBACK BOOKS

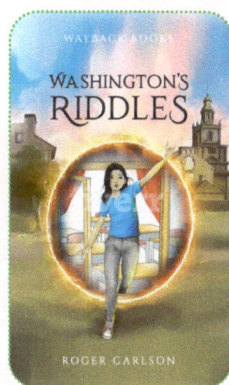
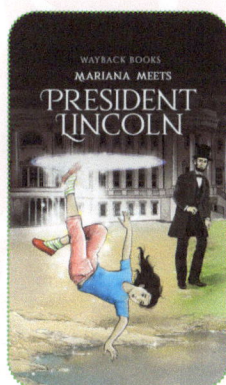
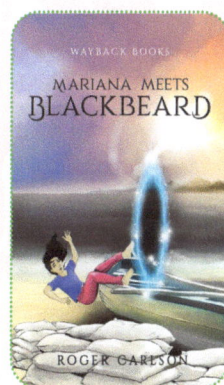

Find us on:

 @marianapublishing   @marianapublishing   @LlcMariana   Mariana Publishing Online

ISBN: 978-1-64510-048-5 (Hardback)
ISBN: 978-1-64510-047-8 (Amazon Paperback)
ISBN: 978-1-64510-049-2 (Print On Demand)

www.ingramcontent.com/pod-product-compliance
Lightning Source LLC
Chambersburg PA
CBHW061051090426
42740CB00002B/111